AF223725

Keats's Anchovy

Keats's Anchovy

By Steve Cranfield

Salt and Honey, with Martin Humphries (poems)

*De purísimo azul / Of Purest Blue, Selected Poems of
Francisco Brines*, with Claudio Tedesco (translation)

F. R. Leavis: The Creative University (criticism)

www.stevecranfield.co.uk

Keats's Anchovy
First published in 2021 by Anchovy Verse, London UK
www.stevecranfield.co.uk

This collection and Introduction © Steve Cranfield 2021
Art © Andrea Aste 2021

The rights of Steve Cranfield to be identified as the author of this work have been asserted by him in accordance with the Copyright, Designs and Patents Act of 1988.

All rights reserved. No part of this publication may be reproduced, stored in a retrieval system, or transmitted, in any form or by any means electronic, photocopying, recording or otherwise, without the prior written permission of the publisher or a license permitting copying in the UK by the Copyright Licensing Agency Ltd (www.cla.co.uk), except by a reviewer, who may quote brief passages in a review.

ISBN 978-1-7399301-0-3

Cover, art, and book design by Andrea Aste
www.andreaaste.co.uk

Keats's Anchovy

Steve Cranfield

Nunca un buen lector de poesía será un ciudadano fanático

Francisco Brines

A good reader of poetry will never be a bigoted citizen

Some of these poems first appeared in: *RFD*; *Salt and Honey* (with Martin Humphries, Gay Men's Press); *Barzakh*; and *Of Eros and of Dust* (edited by Steve Antony) and *Jugular Defences* (edited by Peter Daniels and Steve Antony), both with the Oscars Press.

'Tina and Joan and Don and Karl' was written for an evening of poetry and performances at the Diorama, 9 January 1990, to help raise funds for ACT UP London to continue its campaign of direct action to end the AIDS crisis.

'Post Mortem Effects' and 'Rabbit Out of Hiding': thank you to Piotr Drukier for letting me use some of our conversations in these poems.

Contents

Notes

Art

15

Introduction

This book of new and selected poems brings together the titular 'Keats's Anchovy' and four sequences arranged chronologically from 1987 to the present. What connects these sets of poems, very different in form and subject? My candidate for a unifying theme is what a character in one of the poems calls 'the ordinary real'. Readers will of course form their own impressions, aided (I trust) by Andrea Aste's delightful images, which enter into thematic dialogue with each section.

The sonnet sequence 'The Day the Earth Stood Still' is the earliest. It treads a well-worn path of romantic love from first flush to bum's rush. If the route is familiar it's hoped the reader will gain a fresh angle on the staging-posts: excitement, euphoria, feelings of doubt and anxiety, followed by the inevitable licking of wounds. I once invited the beautiful, elusive fellow Irishman who inspired these poems to a reading at which I hoped he would be stung by remorse. Wisely, he phoned the venue at the last minute to send his apologies.

'Chrysleriana' was written on visits as a health educator to New York City at the height of the AIDS epidemic. I was allowed privileged entry into the worlds of individuals living with HIV, including fellow gay men, drug users and those in recovery, many of them Black or Hispanic. I wanted to record, in however minimal a way, their courage, generosity, dignity and feistiness. Two poets, Federico García Lorca and my friend the late Assotto Saint (1957-94), are the companions at the opening and close of the sojourn in this beautiful, brutal city.

'Homage to Isabel Rawsthorne' aims to reverse the method of 'art in dialogue with poetry' referred to above with Andrea Aste. Before 2021 my knowledge of Rawsthorne was confined to her as the subject of Bacon's magisterial portraits. Her commitment as an artist in her own right to perceiving 'the ordinary real' in our bodily experience of the world struck a chord.

'Horse Head of the Moon Goddess' brings together recent poems about art, politics and family.

The book contains numerous birds and beasts. Some are hunters, some are hunted, some are consumed. One creature gets top billing. I could offer many reasons for my fondness for the anchovy, beyond its surprising mildness when fresh: its elegant, compact shape, its sheen, its association with plenty (*abbondanza*), its freely-moving vitality that takes it foraging into most waters of the planet. But its poignant, love-hate relationship with the dying Keats is the clincher. Keats described himself as a chameleon poet; perhaps in his final days in Rome, when this venturesome fish unexpectedly found its way to his table, as the only form of daily sustenance allowed by the medics, he was also part-anchovy.

Steve Cranfield

London, 29 July, 2021

Keats's Anchovy

Keats's Anchovy

As if the refusal to give him laudanum,
the bleeding for curative purposes,
the quarantine in Naples aboard ship,
the late arrival in Rome when warm weather
had passed, the hacking cough, the fevers, night sweats,
tenacious sputum that clawed the roof of his mouth,
the blood-soaked lint (arterial, he knew it),
the patter of feet, not tiny, street cries
that spoke in accents that were not hers,
were not enough, they decided to restrict him
to an anchovy and a crust of bread a day.
They'll say they probably knew no better, those days,
but wasn't this the case, even back then?
There but for the grace, a cautionary tale,
but cautioning against what, or whom, exactly?

Forget the aesthete's relish, the vinaigrette,
the zest of lemon and the zest for life.
Forget the snack, the titbit, antipasti.
Imagine this is the zenith of your day,
your cracked lips perform their open sesame,
your tongue makes contact with a sleek thin fish,
silvery-grey, white-bellied, with a tang
and taste at which you must feel an aching
gratitude. Multiply this by as many
times as they place it before you until
the sight of this dead creature draped over bread,
like some slinky fur stole dropped on a chaise longue,
without even a hint of drizzled oil,
has you doubting the wisdom of reading
ever again the miracle of abundance
of the loaves and fishes. You would happily

stop at the two, and call it a lucky
coincidence, accept that the crucifixion
is promise enough without this specious
bribe of resurrection. Wasn't it Christ
risen himself who offered them a grilled fish?
'What have you got to eat?' Rubbing it in.

But look at it from the anchovy's perspective.
Your fated honour to sustain this husk,
if only for an instant, or before he retched.
Caution and risk held no meaning for you
as you swam into the net along with
thousands of others exactly like you,
schooled in obedience and nothing more,
selected by hands unknown to be
a soothing second in a life of agony
in the gullet of a dying foreigner,
ending up as projectile vomit or shit,
tossed in the river, thence towards the sea
you came from, less than a day before,
your innards, spine and head taking a little
longer to get there via the local cat,
your will having played no part, absolved
from blame in being taken in, spat out,
or purged to the sound of a strange tongue,
despite your celebrated mildness,
to have been the occasion, to have touched,
however briefly, a poet's throat.

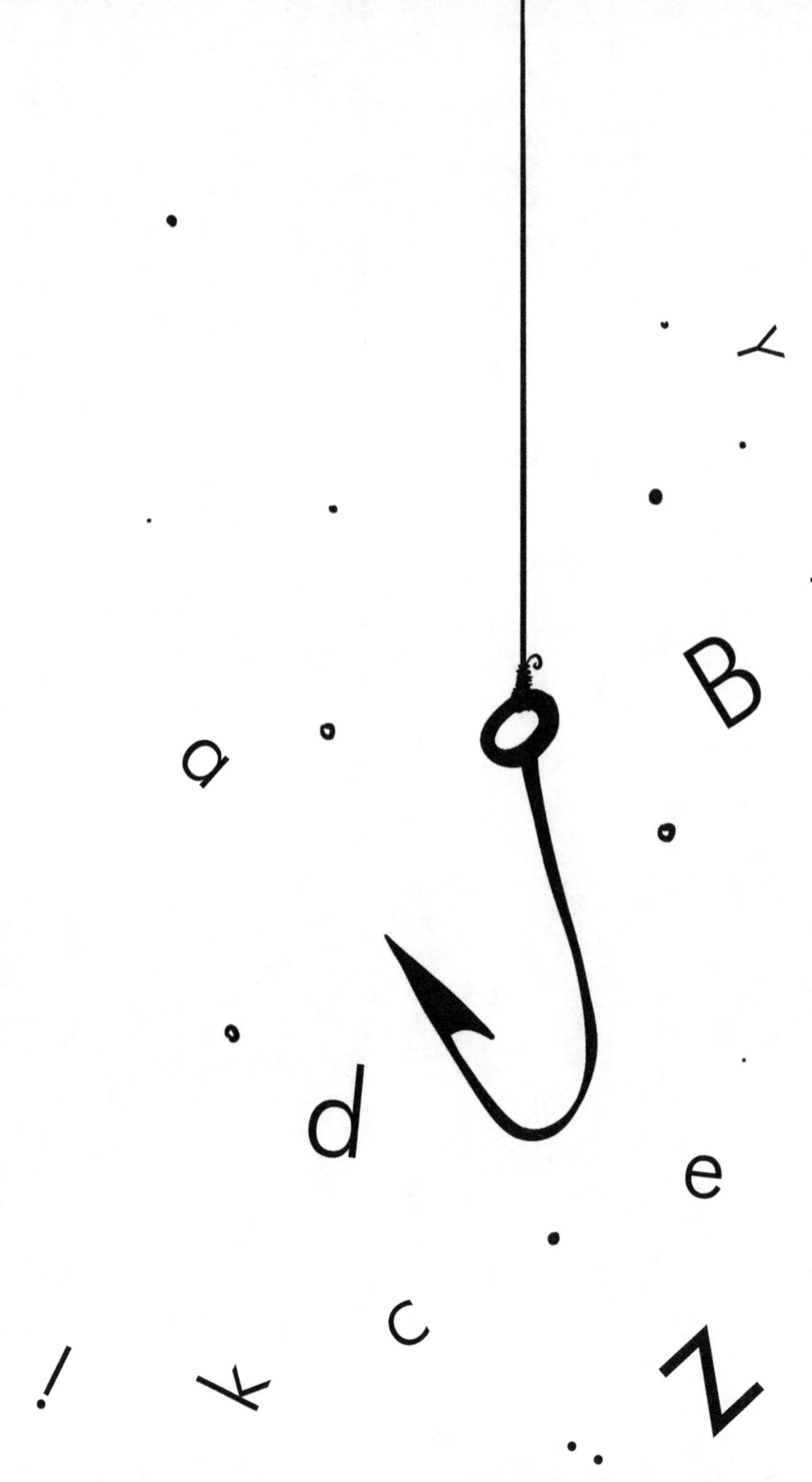

The Day the Earth Stood Still

You scroungy bastard, you hot bloody moose.

Mark Ameen, *Those of You Who Are Dying Are Very Gifted*

The Day the Earth Stood Still

For Mark Ameen

In the '50s' sci-fi movie of that name,
Klaatu arrives smoothly by flying saucer,
bringing peace to the States – but with, of course, a
10 ft. minder robot, Gort, in tow (tame
as a toy till riled). There's always some damn
trigger-happy jerk decides to force a
showdown – you know, the sweaty het, the coarser
G.I. who mows down aliens, blacks, the same.
Klaatu gets shot (what else?): Gort goes berserk.
The earthling heroine alone's been taught to
say the code that halts its mayhem; will it work?
Love, be my Gort, you 6 ft. killer, stick to
your guns despite a voice that stutters *Klaatu
barada nikto … Klaatu barada nikto …*

To Speke of Wo That Is in Mariage

'When sorrows come they come not single spies
but in battalions.' It's the same with men,
or used to be: make love one day in ten,
or twenty, once you're coupled in the eyes
of others – friends, you fuck all day, despise
a bed that's ever made, express a yen
for croissants under covers. Night again –
you're hot, twined, kissing the joy as it flies.
They say the same of buses: was there ever
a throng of red arrivals like his love?
Or such a gap as followed? You could sever
connections, trust a piercing motive, move,
or stay and watch the rust creep up the knife,
and have, like Valium, a long half-life.

Hic Est Corpus Meum

For Steve, Ronnie and Sandro

'Thank God for what you get, there's thousands dying
in Africa. It does, it breaks His heart
to see you pushing food around the plate –
it's a mortal sin, you know, to leave food lying
there, going stone cold. And it's no good trying
to say you've had enough. Kids! So ungrate-
ful these days … My mother would throw a fit!'
Perverse refusals set me off defying
social conventions: food first, then good-bye
religion; marriage; last, monogamy –
plant-eating, atheist, gay, promiscuous, sinner!
My lips; his prick: my teeth just grazed the shaft as
I became the boy, half-way through his dinner –
all I could do was think of 'What's for afters?'

Give Me Back My Man

In memoriam Ricky Wilson

I have a secret love. My heart is burning.
But will he play the game? I know some tricks.
I'll fall into his strong arms like a fix.
I'll stir some unmet, deep, unconscious yearning
in his man's breast. Passion will mount. Tides turning.
His swelling manhood pressed. To mine. Limbs mix.
He'll see the light. (I've known since I was six.)
All parts rhyme. Yearning, burning and returning.
Surrendering the all I have to give.
I've got you under my skin. Now each day's
dawning will bring discoveries, new ways
to mesh us. Never split. Infinitive.
Vows, hearts, exchanged. We'll die of love. Clichés,
like viruses, need our fresh blood to live.

Tree-Names

Ponga   Pohutukawa   Nikau   Sounds
of strange antipodean trees I brought
back, as well as photos and a tan (caught
with a will that could last me fifteen rounds).
That night we found each other, stripped and amazed,
I pulled out souvenirs of foreign parts,
more to vacate us, I suspect, from hearts
too near to leaking, than to prompt your dazed
admiring of the white streak round my waist.
Maybe the print of sun on flesh defines
the love of men. If not that, music: just
a deep voice singing to a plain guitar
some long and moody cantilena lines.
Kauri   Totara   Kowhai   Manuka

ponga: pron. *punga*
kowhai: pron. *kohfeye*

Hanging on the Telephone

You won't find anyone living inside
my pockets, and I've had the breast one stitched!
I'm generous, but no mug, I won't be hitched
on the basis of one measuring night. Wide
open my arms may be but … All the more
surprising then that I should start to feel
possessed/possessive in your absence, real
in your dreams, my teased skin tugging the core.
I'm not so rigid that I can't admit
impediments to speaking that ur-phrase,
so groomed love's understudy to displace
the lame yet stubborn star (who knows he's had it) …
With you I entertained a high-matching hope:
I came a poor third behind the coke and dope.

Gym Class of '67
(Summer of Love)

How it was. Pat Stack, lanky, loth to wear
a top, his tight shorts always lingering
over slim hips. Pat Shallow, coal black hair
in curls, pellucid nipples blistering
his marble pecs. Geoff Tompkins, tanned broad chest,
the first to flaunt an adult's cock and bush.
Paul Grubiak, in many ways the thickest,
fore and aft. Steve Cranfield, needing a push
to lose his vest. Kev Hartnett, smart Y-fronts,
easing his balls into their soft white pouch.
Dick Green, gym master, sunning himself once
on pitch (not showering, alas!). To touch
this side of sweaty sleep proving unable …
Writing, one hand still gropes beneath the table.

Clean Slates

Love, like construction, calls for many talents:
hard graft; an eye for physical relations;
style; tolerance of mess; a sense of balance;
a head for heights; a nose for firm foundations.
That summer was a neat repair man's act.
Your touch was felt from cellar up to eave.
You braved loose scaffolding, at last attacked
the damage nesting birds and weather leave.
Despite the fact that you denied the claim
love can provide a long-term dwelling place,
I made you master-builder all the same,
asked for four walls round my potential space.
I couldn't trust love's craft, I needed proof.
From you I learnt how not to tile a roof.

Rules of the Game

I'm into pain, I must be or I guess
I'd stop handcuffing us in poetry,
making us Ms to serve love's mighty S.
That's tough on you, true, tougher still on me.
They say that fantasy's O.K. so long
as it's made solo or consensual,
but where's the safety in a top who's strong
on bullshit, rules the memory as well?
I kiss his boots, he's swift to punish failure,
talks dirty ... Yet, I can't help thinking how,
for all the worn bondage paraphernalia,
he couldn't yoke us then, can't hold you now.
You cut clean through these words like a machete:
the tender poems monotonous confetti.

The First Law of Thermodynamics

You're hot, man: the effect of ethanol?
Or ultra-violet light? (My words, perhaps?)
You're the front-runner after fifteen laps,
the oven gas mark 9, Nevada soil.
Mercury from its bulb is inching tall,
twin phallic symbols mosey on down their flaps
(acetyl choline flooding every synapse):
they mount, they shine, evaporate and fall …
Systems approaches engineer a crisis
(this humid atmosphere inhibits sweat),
potentiate the feedback of desire:
don't starve this fever, don't encourage lysis.
You're hot, man, but not overheating, yet …
Just light the blue touch-paper and retire.

Carpe Diem

In memoriam Bobby Reynolds

You haven't any time to spin conundrums
disguising identities of your lover ...
So many men, so little time: that syndrome's
out too, good memories are in. Crab mover,
career change cannot grab you any longer.
You haven't any time for songs that boast
Die young stay pretty, you've gotta live fast
cause it won't last.[1] Time's halt's where you belong, a
double region filled with hiatuses
of dreams and poems (fuck- or otherwise),
creating spaces, filling in those gaps,
turning your blind eye, limping, deaf and dumb.
This urgency is unangelic: perhaps
that's where the poem comes. Or does not come.

[1] Deborah Harry

Tristana, o la Historia del Amor

12 strokes. The bell clapped by a severed head.
But that's to spoil the ending. Let's go back
to the point where a dog's sudden attack
on Tristana's heel (an amputated
leg the consequence) makes for a scene change.
She hobbles through part 2. Should we applaud
as vile Don Lope, paralysed in bed,
asks for more warmth but suffers cool revenge?
She brings no comfort, precious little hope, and
lets the snow pile in. And she doesn't laugh.
His body, like her heart, freezes to death.
'I haven't seen *Tristana* since it opened …
I remember liking the second half.'
(Chapter 20, Buñuel's *My Last Breath*)

Pulp Horror

It is a living force which can be tapped
at any given moment of the night.
Its most feared colour is unblemished white.
To every climate change it can adapt
and call to regions still by hand unmapped.
It dazzles with huge vistas (this despite
the rough draughts blowing leaves across your sight),
pipes flawless tunes: no single note is scrapped.
It lives off forests, drinks your sacred sweat,
and promises to wipe clean every debt:
You are my chosen, my original.
Two simple words will banish it, and yet
you dare not use them, you are in its thrall.
It is the most dangerous game of all.

Ad Hominem

Men don't go off sex for no good reason.
I want instruction – while spare logic shows
our pricks for the gristle they are, mine grows
up demanding on every occasion
his muscular sibling: not that I need
repeat synchronised duets, like mechanical
raised leaves of a bridge – just beat that tyrannical
dick! Voicing which didn't make his heart bleed –
the effect or lack of one, intended –
or interrupt his morning homage to
the weed. Only the smoke-rings that he blew
linked us, too cool by then to say he'd ended.
Which was the more to blame, it's hard to say.
My fetters? His *Noli me tangere*?

In Truth the Prison

Nuns fret not at their convent's narrow room;
And hermits are contented with their cell.
Intrusions of privacy yet to come,
such could have been our forecast fate as well.
To shadow forth ideal communion,
to rouse the nation, capture agapē
(in 14 lines) or woo the younger man
with promises of fame beyond today,
were honourable trades for antique sonnets.
Small wonder I chose (had chosen for me?)
a verse form that's gasping for air, that's on its
last legs, to celebrate love that hardly
learnt to crawl, let alone walk. A safe bet
that Wordsworth never met a nun. They fret.

Livre pour Orchestre

Like settling an old score on the piano,
my practised hands are moving on the quiet.
Shadows dissolve, the lord of black and white
keys into tones that only he can know.
Voices on darkness: can these lips astound
eyes more-or-less dilatory? Two lines merging
underscore faint trust? Or is this me verging
on white noise, making overtones to sound?
I lack the necessary orchestrative
skill (granted): here mouth-music is the best.
I know you through no eye – each fading look,
untrained, no longer reads you like a book –
so whisper phrases: the sound operative
only as wooden oblongs are depressed.

On Not Reaching Twenty

Sonnets that never get beyond their teens
can seem cut short (harsh fate now intervenes),
14 plus 3 a radical surprise
avoidance of the adult enterprise.
One onlie begetter inspired a hymn to plenty
but the solemn pose had gone by no. 20.
I'm voicing love absurd, whose final twist
restores to me a sense too long dismissed.
I'm missing you, too tense to make an ending,
live love-bait out to hook, tough lines suspending.
This says too much: enclosed within our sex is
power to clinch that third decade (2 exes).
Pardon this close – the fault all mine not yours –
and think what only once: no cause, no cause.

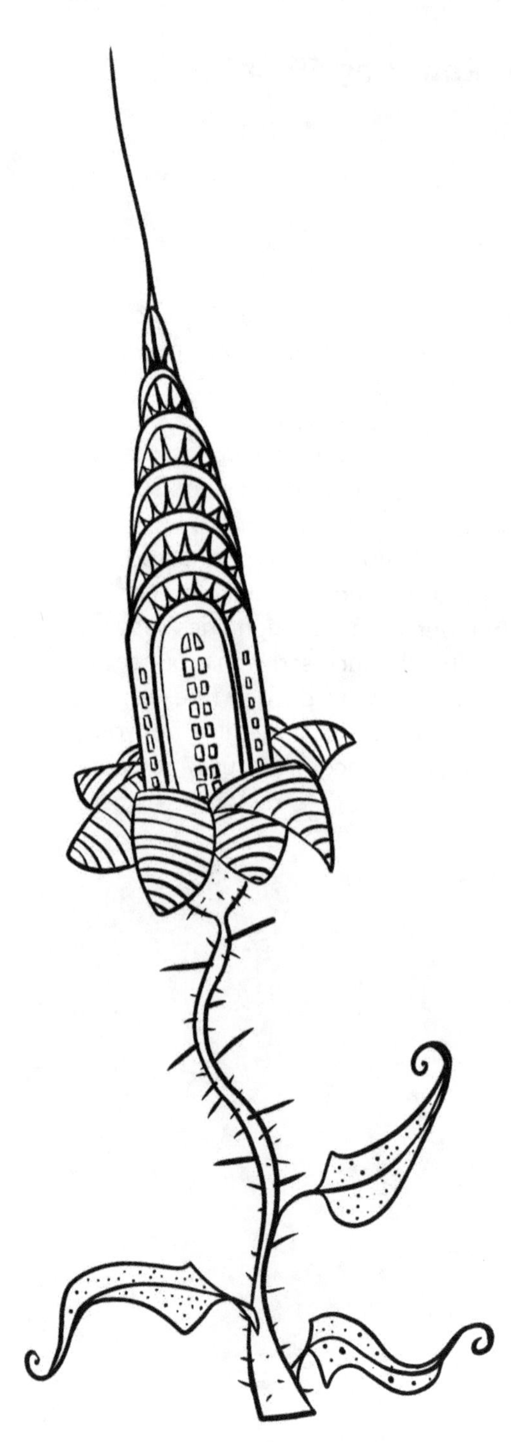

Chrysleriana

Grito hacia la Torre del Crysler Building (desde Islington)

Here you see the typist with fabulous legs that we have seen in so many films.

Lorca, letter from New York to his family, 1929

Perched on Columbia's pile, room 617,
you sit stylites, athlete of god, your tongue's
deep blue denied, fed by a dream, your waking sense
picking up lumpen phonemes with castrated tongs.

The tree in the garden holds fruit of stainless steel.
Everyone knows gum, the fabulous legs of typists,
no one sings crystals in the powderless air,
no one draws steam across languages of tea-chests.

You write home: 'There'd be no use my trying to express...'
Or one part of you does, 'the foreigner'. The other
sees compressed air turning on red detonations,
the Bronx kids stripped to the waist, earth seeking its father,

the churches squeezed into place like furniture,
a tinsel virgin assassinated by the sky.
'Everything human, everything soothing, everything
beautiful is suppressed.' You sense the familial lie.

No one waits in hours of black rings and linen,
no one trusts roses or an apple in his bed.
When two supple limbs fret the strings of your heart,
what chords are broken, what secrets are unsaid?

Daffodils glow in grey corners of the room.
Four-thirty a.m.: who lies beside you now, who had
the darkest kiss piercing beneath the pillow?
What your body tells you is of no dying god.

Planned Decay

'The odds against meeting someone in N.Y.
are extremely great, as great as two fish
meeting in the open sea.' On a northbound train
past Yankee Stadium the odds for diminish

even further: 'probably best experienced
only as a passing cityscape
from the relative comfort of the subway.'
Seating in stalls allows the eye no escape

from blinded tenements, odd wisps of smoke,
rusted cans, burnt-out cars, every cliché
of urban deprivation, all except
the intentional: this is 'planned' decay.

And I can offer no consoling childhood
interlude, fantasy's attic where you
shift the scene, no Poem of Eight-Years-Old,
'Those eyes of mine in 1962 ...,'

to wish this sight away, having been raised
on West Ham ash: the triangle between Berk
Chemicals, the northern sewer outfall
and the bomb-site of Memorial Park,

where the Three Mills River's dull copper snake
wound over ooze between a black-walled canyon,
aerials fought with precocious dioxides,
and stuttering first steps in the dawn

kicked up a sulphurous dew ... My attention
strays to within the carriage, and to feet:
the Reebok-quotient still seems pretty high.
I'm looking up, at the man sitting opposite

since 167th St.,
a largish parcel balanced on his knees.
He meets my glance. His right hand gently moves
to open his leather jacket. His eyes freeze.

His belt displays a bayonet knife. He smiles ...
Burnside Avenue. He's edging to the doorway.
It sighs open. Shut. He weaves south, below.
Through glazed eyes I see him swim away.

In Defence of Deborah Harry

Open Auden or Tony Harrison's
latest and you're sure to find yet another
cheap side-swipe at the home of fast-food chains,
Fatburgers, Hungry Horse, the Tummy Stuffer.
Those horny Hollywoods, etc.
Slagging the States cuts your satiric teeth
or dentures. Envy? Or superior
dishonesty to claim that it's beneath
us to acknowledge our m/paternity?
Where I grew up the phrase 'like a bomb's hit it'
was no simile but reality:
escaped this devastation as the minder
to those who, likewise, need no such defender.
'I'm not livin' in the real world'[1]: admit it!

[1] Jimmy Destri

City of Dead Umbrellas

On Lexington/East 74th St.
much delayed municipal cleansing weather
assists dried blood to quit the sidewalk. Beet-
root stains are polished off by Gucci leather:
yesterday's oxblood toned down to maroon.
Showers have sprouted an umbrella stall
by an awning: $8 each, but soon
prices, like rain, chance periodic fall
to 6, 4. 'No-one, but no-one, goes out
carrying one of those things rolled up here,
unless he's expecting trouble, and not
from the elements.' The discarded fear
litters the streets: black viscose, wind-blown sticks,
bats pinned to the ground by hypodermics.

Chrysleriana

Is it silly or is it real?

Paul Goldberger, on the Chrysler Building

I

Daily forays you made at sidewalk level
but each dusk found you homing on those neon
portals, to savour the experience,
much as Q the Winged Serpent, hatched by heat, set free on

rooftop bathers ('Maybe his head just got loose
and fell off'), retired at night to dine.
Rituals? Reconditioned junk? Or both?
And would you buy a used car from this man?

II

'Los hombres deben usar condones
en sus relaciones sexuales,'
the subway ads enjoin the young Hispanics,
the Protestant ethic, ever pleasureless,

their doom translating: 'Es possible que
usted ya tiene AIDS y no lo sabe.'
When their green speech assumes majority
one loving ally more, not less, maybe.

III

A methadone clinic at Montefiore,
the Bronx: this morning's subject safer sex
education. 'What's the best way, Rosaura,
what's a sure way to bring a john to climax

in under five minutes? Better still, what'll make
him shoot his load before he gets inside? …
Peer group pressure!' 'How comes Francisco gets
to use this place when he's doing shit?' 'I tried

to clean up, twice, my lady wouldn't let me.
We got three kids. They eat. What kind of steady
job would bring me this much cash, respect?'
Whatever might be said's been said already.

Tina and Joan and Don and Karl

Tina said to me: 'We've been doing our act
for two years now. At first, we were amateurs,
then we got coaching from a Method actor.
He's hot, but all the material is ours,

he just helps us put it across. It's based
on true incidents, they really happened
to Joan and me, and Don and Karl.
In between skits we do our rap:

"Don't/share/your works (let me hear you say it)/
don't/share/your works (let me hear you say it)/
don't share your needle/your cotton or spoon/
or you'll have some trouble that's coming real soon/

find a way to cook it that's safe/there's a way/
or you'll be cooking an AIDS soufflé.
Don't/share/your works (let me hear you say it)/
don't/share/your works (let me hear you say it)/

DON'T/SHARE/YOUR WORKS."'
                              Joan said to me: 'We do
our skits in front of welfare workers, showing
the kinds of things they do to addicts, the way
we're always last in line for everything,

and then there's nothing left, the quiet way
you tell the social worker, "I have AIDS,"
and he says, "Fill this form in first please (lady),"
the way the clinic nurse looks heavenwards,

and says, "You junkies should be sterilised."
We change attitudes. Some people cry.
It's time they started. We used to do sessions
one a week, that was before Don and me

got sick. We had your British TV here
last year, wanting to film us shooting up.
We're clean! There always is a TV crew here,
the wired-up chasing the wired-up,

this place makes more money as a film lot.
We bring our daughter with us on these jaunts,
she knows the scripts by heart. Some say the children
follow in the footsteps of the parents,

but who do we leave her with? Some people here
you couldn't trust with your dog. Loco?
Their brains are fried! Besides, she ought to know
what's going on. Everyone ought to know.'

Don said nothing to me.
                    Karl said to me:
'First they said, "You need a group." Group? What group?
There is no group, unless you're referring
to the waiting room. So they said, "Start one up."

Start one up? I need a home, one with a *roof*!
"That proves our point," they said. And the point is of …?
"You just get angry with us all the time,
you're leaking feelings more than the roof.

You need a group." Groups will empower you,
they said. You hear us say that sometimes too,
especially in groups, not just in line
for methadone each day. But this is no

Manhattan, this is Beirut. No one gets
released till they force the City to start
handing out needles and the megabucks.
Meanwhile, the hostages are sweating it out.

You're luckier than we were, you got time.
Talk to Don. He can put it better than me.
He writes the lyrics, not just protest poems,
he *is* expression.'
                    Don said nothing to me.

Triple Mysteries

For Assotto Saint

I

You'd had enough, had started giving a miss
to services since the twelfth man in your building
went: 'The tears were for myself.' So, instead,
you paid your respects to Sun and Moon, holding

the rituals of Amun, Mut and Khon,
a nuclear family wise enough to dwell
invisible on east and western banks,
hidden in names, but summoned by a spell

at noontide in an unusual alphabet,
convinced that nothing less than absolute
necessity of miracle could chase
America's brutal, evil spirits out ...

Seeking to learn by heart the awkward names:
Dweller within the Cavern of the Lord,
She who foretells Mornings throughout her Life,
Mistress of Darkness, Foremost, Dancing on Blood,

Piercing of Voice, Flint Sharpener, Lover of Heat,
Mistress of Anger, Scorcher of Rebels, Dread,
She above whom Osiris stretches his Arms,
the twenty-one secret portals of the dead ...

A Nubian queen danced naked on a roof,
hotter than sand and the tarmac melting on it,
among the tenements between B and C,
descended through the starry cool of granite,

past the twelve pylons of the underworld,
reserved for different eyes and other tongues,
Khepri emerging as the sun again,
his oiled chest bearing talismanic songs.

II

I'd had enough of waiting for the count
to start: 'The fears are for myself.' We strolled
back from the Village, hot. You pointed out
the not-so-empty storerooms where they held

the jack-off parties, venues where the perfected
etiquette of untouchability
held sway, over swaying hands, not holding hips.
You mourned the loss of possibility ...

Meeting, we'd exchanged poems. Force of habit?
Tokens of mutual trust? Civility?
Or evidence of the separate answers that
your Haitian and my Irish family

compelled? I couldn't have said which then.
Ten months on I treasure the cover photo
of you and Jan straddling the globe, the message:
'Dearest Steve: Dare, Dare & Dare. Assotto.'

III

So Scoithín met with Barra long ago:
Barra was in a ship while Scoithín, he
was walking on the sea. Barra would know:
'How can a man be walking on the sea?'

'Green wilderness of earth, not waterscape,'
said Scoithín, as his fingers netted quick
a flower, hauled, and threw it on board ship:
at Barra's feet a poppy on the deck.

'How can a ship go floating on a field?'
asked Scoithín. Barra's hand plunged through the spray,
plucked out a fish, and shed it on the field:
at Scoithín's feet a salmon on the clay.

Homage to Isabel Rawsthorne

Green Woodpecker III, 1946

An *objet trouvé* or *objeu*, the space
between word and thing, the play of the mind:
a solitary male, frozen in snow,
on a winter's walk, hung against white board.

'Describe the tongue of a woodpecker,'
wrote Leonardo, as a way of training
the eye. Don't just look at things, scrutinise.
Note how far it retracts inside the skull.

What he took for granted was finding the bird,
holding one in the hand, transporting it,
having a place to bring it back to, having
a light source, materials, time. You didn't.

Nor was your goal that of mere description.
Once thawed, you unfolded its wings like a fan,
moss green to charcoal, white radial dabs,
string tied round one claw, yellow rump askew.

That was description good (or bad) enough.
Suspended head down, words like swoop, dive, fall,
said nothing. What mattered was presence, not likeness,
of this orphaned Icarus minus the wax.

Lizard, 1946

We both have
four limbs,
a head,
eyes, nostrils,

a spine
that widens,
a mouth that can stay
shut.

My toes too
have been
known in their time
to splay.

Shifting the weight
from one foot
to the other,
child's play.

Under certain conditions
I also can assume
a tinge of green,
a passable yellow.

I even have
tucked away somewhere
the memory
of a tail.

But the maroon
baked earth
you lie on
and make love to,

straddling the cracks,
goes to show
how little
we've in common.

Your torso
that twists
a full
ninety degrees

says you'll have
none of me,
insists you're
unbefriendable.

Three Fish, 1948

The fish are framed in a quadrangular grid,
as on an identification chart.
No fisherman, I'd hazard they are pollocks.
The one on top heads downward purposely.
The middle, by contrast, does its scaly job
of floating, effortless reflection. The maturest
below, with a strong underbite, thrusts its head
in an oxblood square, the black-on-white eye
an arresting full stop for fish and viewer.

The pollock life cycle? Not much to deduce
here. And to say the most developed returns
an inquisitive stare would be absurdly
anthropomorphic, the painting implies.
Yet it stares, as doubtless did the painter.
And a form of communication opens up.
Not just from its lustrous fishy existence
or its modern milieu but from a shared
Palaeozoic past, a life pared down.

The Desert, 1948-50

Seeing someone from a distance, known or unknown,
fortuitous or expected, how revealing it was,
for a city dweller, including the non-average,
against a backdrop with more gaps than usual.

True, there was the straight street, the open square,
the bridge, the river perhaps, but not
the bare hill, long shore, lane, cart, open field,
to frame an approach, departure, passing by.

Hence the desert, not characterised as
arid, unoccupied, devoid of life and colour –
there are two birds arising, a woman walking:
'the dark green light at midday,' you described it.

Not unproductive either. What would happen
if one's vision sought not the easel picture
but the straight-on, left and right, did away with
those cherished customs, landmarks, three dimensions?

Dead Hare, 1951

In times of rationing how long can you afford
to paint in oils an edible still life subject?
Long enough to record its boxing pose before
it hits the pot: a persistent buck, or a doe
past provocation. Palate, palette, coincide.
Realising the recipe, method, those matter.
Don't spare a thought for cleaning up after yourself.

Untitled (Owl), c. 1950-60

Too late to
backtrack
swerve avoid

dispondic
straight-on
left right

great wings
beating still
above the

staggering
terrified
loosening

by the time you catch its eye
your name's been gutted

Baboon, 1962

Crouching, cornered, Rodin's *Thinker* pose,
scarcely discernible, grey-blue ochre shade.

Bull of the baboons,
governing the dark.

Thrice confined, by cage, frame, glass,
the fathomed eye.

It's been a while since he returned the viewer's gaze.
Each seems to be blurrily at a loss.

Is he really thinking? Really mourning?
These are prose questions, not the painting's.

As if you could draw a straight line between
baboon-mourning and human-mourning.

What does this mourning require of us, exactly?
This is the more interesting consideration.

It is the difference between
having a smart answer at the ready

and attending to the question
'What meaning-mourning could exist among baboons?'

It is the difference, the painting shows,
between solitude and solicitude.

Migration V, c. 1970s

It might from the look of it
be Dupuytren's contracture,
your right hand fingers
bent towards the palm.

Or maybe you're practising
your bowing technique,
never forgetting that
each and every finger

is an individual,
apart from the crowd,
not thumb on the bottom,
the rest on top.

Hands, solar and lunar,
swaddle a swallow,
one heading right,
one heading left,

a fleeting detention
by human interest.
A sombre plesiosaur,
wedged in the blue,

its fossil arrangement
tells a further story,
of once marine movement:
we won't be here long.

Migration VI, c. 1970s

Yes, writers can write by hand, and leave
a mark on paper. Some even leave tear stains.
And manuscripts provide fertile fodder
for fingerprint forensics. You instead
leave a record of the image of your hand,
the one that shaped the image that we see
or maybe the one that didn't wield the brush.

Not just a signature motif, applied
after the event, or a metaphor
for self-portraiture only, but the back
or front of a rough pink mottled hand,
held upright at arm's distance, the fingers
splayed for curiosity, defiance, wonder.
Or just for the record. Yes, that will do.

Stoats and Moon, c. 1985

no swallow in the stack sign me to leap

But the stoats do still,
have done for a decade,
understudies to Nureyev:
you of all should know,
you've sketched him too.

They arc across a pale moon,
as in *La Bayadère*,
coming in for a landing,
on what we can't tell.
No stoat leaps for joy.

Sparrowhawk, c. 1990

Glean from the symbol
its hinterland in Egypt,
    then come back home.

Place the bird high up,
spread wings
    unwavering, off-centre.

Avoid any suggestion
of the dove,
    the redemptive.

Imply the world below
in the posture
    of its head.

Give it tail feathers
long and tapering,
    unshaken by wind.

Inscribe the characters
of those who have touched you
    with their hands.

Scratch faintly in the paint
the names of four
    artists, poets, friends.

Incise more distinctly
il prenome of another:
    love's glyph.

Return the recalled gesture.
Leave fingerprint traces
        of charcoal dust.

Choose carefully the sky
from Pantone's many.
        Accord it no conquest.

Celeste polvere,
pallido,
        velato,

powdery,
pale,
        overcast blue.

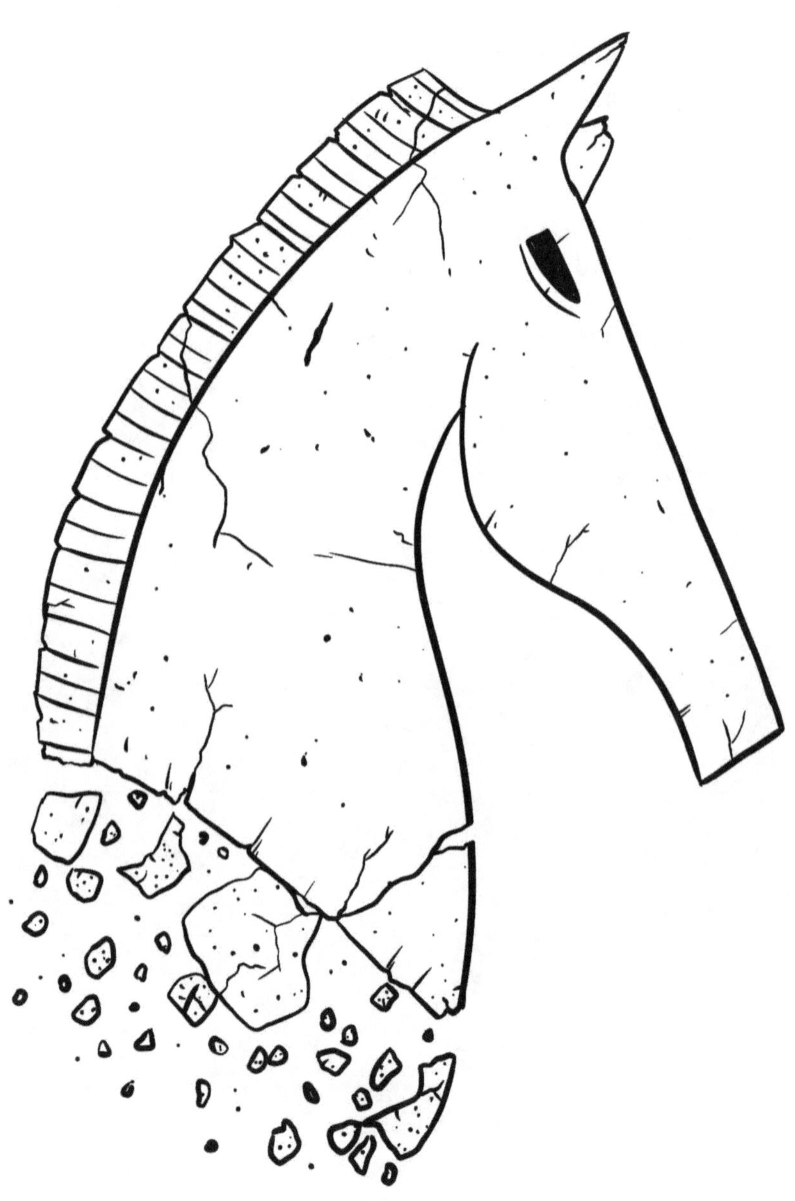

Horse Head of the Moon Goddess

Impersonating a Cuckoo

After Gustave Courbet's 'Still Life with Apples and a Pomegranate'

Whoever imagined that a red hot poker,
spikes at the ready, with its upright torch,
might shoo away the dark battalions
through quantitative easing, summon larks,
shape windows towards the east, place a dish
just so, with towered walnuts, orchard apples,
lolling pomegranate cuckooing beneath
for good measure, whoever assumed that
joy was anything but a mild surprise,
like the print of sun on the back of a hand
or a Greek tomato split open to reveal
a crimson deep as any strawberry,
knew little of the essence of dejection,
you concluded. Best to rely on tactics
of sound, not simply those of human voices,
loved or familiar, or both, or neither,
one-two-*three*-four-and-*five*-six-*seven*-eight,
Sophia Loren's cha-cha-cha, or mambo,
but empty vessels struck, bristle of bamboo
and other proxies of the fidgety wind.
Avoid the artificial harbingers,
trombone or telephone, loud or frail,
oompah oompah, ting-a-ling-ling:
no poem would survive its sound effects.

Picasso's Prostate

He'd have a gentle morning. Canvas drying.
Where to account for this truly masculine
organ? Never mind the gilded phalloi,
the chiselled pecs, the wizened dugs, the delts,
where was the prostate gland in art?

The secret, secretive gland that once
propelled his semen up a standing mirror,
the size of a walnut (more like two these days),
the generative organ, why had it
never generated iconography?

After all, it got him out of his bed
more often than smouldering inspiration.
He had a date to sketch a Chinese girl,
two-and-a-half-years old. Most enchanting.
Scheduled for after lunch so she'd be snoozy ...

Failing that, he'd give her and the mother
some dainty sandwiches before the start,
cute little triangles served on black slates,
such as you would get at a *vernissage*.
He always served his female models these,

better than a draught for inducing slumber.
The preponderance of sleeping beauties
in his *oeuvre*, unwoken by a kiss,
the lounging, was merely practical,
a device to fix the sitter, relax the pose.

Not that they were pinioned. This Chinese girl,
take her for instance, like a wounded bird
from human care now disengaged and mad
with flight. That's how he would imagine her
and draw her, as she probably fidgeted

on mum's weary lap. Models scarcely held
a ten-minute pose these days. Then again,
his walnut shared their sense of urgency.
The need to be up and away, to stretch
and yawn, take a leak, rub a stiff knee,

cast shadows in the sun unscrutinised.

Dream of Fair to Middling

You dreamt you were in a group of people
seated outdoors in the sun, among whom
was a very young Samuel Beckett,
dressed smartly in a woollen overcoat.
Very dapper, not in the least forbidding,
other than by glacial reputation.
You were sitting opposite but you'd not been
introduced, let alone exchanged a nod.
Someone said, 'You two should work together,'
a suggestion which Beckett registered
with apparent equanimity.
(Even in your dream you could see where this one
was heading.) People talked of this and that,
how Beckett would never go anywhere
near the Internet: too many writers
having drafts stolen like drawers off the line,
eighty-five percent published without consent.
He was most specific about the percentage
as well as the dinginess of the drawers.
The group broke up and Beckett wandered past
and grazed your shoulder, deliberately.
You took the hint and followed him into
the adjacent pub and as you reached the bar,
Beckett (coolly): 'It's often the case
you end up on different sides of the fence.'
You (nodding): 'The people who are all for freedom
of speech end up by curtailing yours.'
Beckett: 'What did you think of what she said?'
You: 'Which one?' Beckett: 'You don't know?'
That put you in your place. You asked what Beckett
would have: 'A golden sherry.' You leaned over
the bar to the woman serving. She replied:

'Sorry, we do have some other, *ordinary* things.'
End of dream. Beckett left sherryless,
about to be offered some less than gilded
alternative swill. 'The Day I Met Sam.'
Had your dream contrived delivery of
the drink of choice you might have been assured
a place as footnote to the literary greats,
the one to whom the master raised his glass,
if only to inspect the rim for lipstick.

Te Amo Evita

*Para no dejar en pie ningún ladrillo que no sea
peronista.*

Buenos Aires, 1 May 1952

*She's not just the good Evita, the fairy godmother who
gave out toys to children, but a militant Evita committed
to a cause.*

Laura Macek

Two huge forged steel portraits of María Eva
Duarte adorn the north and south facades
of a government ministry midway
down Avenida 9 de Julio,
the widest boulevard in the world,
wide enough for the mass of bodies
your late father-in-law had to step over,

fleeing from the ministry he was visiting
the day the revolution broke in '55.
The portraits, sweet and kick-ass fairy, feature
on many a Tripadvisor bucket list,
along with the Recoleta tomb lodging
the rumoured much-fucked-posthumously corpse.
'Fucked over in death, just like us in life ...'

Your mother-in-law told you that for months
after Evita's funeral all the cafés
and shops had framed photos of *la puta*
with black ribbons. When no one was looking,
she and a friend spat on one. 'She had
her good side, did she? *¡Hija de puta!*'
How they both didn't get shot she'd never know.

Your sister-in-law's mother told you how
one day in the '50s, no day special,
she received a visit from a Peronista
in the hairdressing salon she ran
in one of the barrios where loyalties
were suspect. Why was there no framed
photograph of Evita on the wall?

'Why, should there be?' she answered, baffled,
as she was taking out a client's curlers.
A photograph would be very good for business,
she was told. Surely she could see the sense
in that? At the same time, not having a photo
could be bad for business, very bad.
She didn't need to have that pointed out?

Testing Properties

Being an expert in construction in steel
in a country that built mainly in brick
meant that one's skills were mostly in demand
from the military, which helped to explain
his subsequent decision to train as one
but in the States, as a builder of bridges.

That day in June of the first coup attempt
found him in his unlucky first career:
civil servant in the Ministry of Defence.
Hearing a sound that in later years he would
associate with *Tora! Tora! Tora!*,
he and a colleague peered out of the window.

Whoosh: his colleague's head is no longer there
but guillotined ten storeys down in the plaza.
He made it home past the dead and injured
amassed Perón supporters. His wife noticed
he was trembling. 'You're sweating like a pig.
Take that shirt off now, Miguel, you're drenched.'

He'd later learn to state the wherewithal
of a material known for strength and toughness.
Begin with checking hardness. Press a diamond
pyramid in steel at a specific load.
Measure diagonal of impression
optically. Measure pulling force.

Determine impact toughness by striking
a standard, prismatic, notched sample
with a test swing hammer. Perform at
different temperatures since fragility
increases as temperature falls.
Steel your nerves. Shut your eyes. Disremember.

Eftalou

*Just us two + abt 36 newly arrived refugee women
children men today 11.30 on beach below Eftalou
Lesvos August 10, 2015*

@Steve_Cranfield

Known for its nine interlinking bays,
and used extensively by naturists,
the beach at Eftalou, 'all pebbles, no
facilities,' still made for 'a wonderful
setting … very peaceful and relaxing,'
according to the websites. That morning
a young German woman (textile), the only
other visitor to the bay, bar the odd
Ottoman viper and scorpion,
approached us and inquired, 'What's happening?'
We told her (naked) it was the first dinghy
of the day, expect to see another eight
before the afternoon's out. We wondered
what women stepping ashore in hijabs
would make of two naked men. Perhaps, though,
they had other priorities. The Turkish
smuggler on this side who met the boat
left us in no doubt as he slashed the dinghy
and retrieved the outboard motor for its
next consignment, cursing us from afar,
and waving what looked like a buck knife.
He vanished as quickly as he'd arrived.
A young man, smartly dressed, asked us the way
in English to the nearest transit camp.
He and some thirty others then set off
westwards to Molyvos but not before
they'd checked their mobiles for a signal, shucked
the blue-and-orange Onar life vests. (Onar
means 'dream' in ancient Greek, we were told.)

Other tourists, mainly the English, muttered
about holidays being spoiled, or if
they must make the crossing, pick another beach.
All fell silent as we passed the convoys
of men carrying infants in their arms
in the blistering heat, we in coaches
that were air-conditioned and half-full at most.
That day I tweeted an unpeopled photo:
'On beach at Eftalou Lesvos. Each
life jacket tells a story.' It garnered
two retweets, one like. A drop in the ocean.

Post Mortem Effects

For Piotr

*If the Great White Whale sank the ship of the Great White
Soul in 1851, what's been happening ever since? Post mortem
effects, presumably.*

D. H. Lawrence, 'Herman Melville's "Moby-Dick"'

'How often do officers lie under oath?'
In my experience, albeit limited,
at the far end of the Likert scale.
I'd yet to meet a cop whose testimony
bore much relation to the truth
other than inverted. You, my friend,

had come across just one, in Bosnia
where he was in charge of identifications
in Krajina – 'the only decent cop
I ever met, twenty years back.' As to what's
been happening since: our reading –
Democracy Now! and Herman Melville.

Post mortem can be a messy business,
you, your forensic pathology hat on,
remind me, by its very nature deadly.
Maybe, you add, stressing 'some', we can
take some comfort in the survival
of some minor things, like some freedoms,

in jars of formalin. 'Handle with caution'
will be printed on each jar, and some jars
will be broken, specimens lost, and with time
and lack of conservation even the best specimens,
like whale flesh opened to the air, will rot
and degrade, secrete great sunken souls.

Rabbit Out of Hiding

*Diversification, liquidity and returns – explore how gold
could enhance your portfolio.*

World Gold Council

What algorithm was it had determined
this 'promoted' item should burrow down
quite snugly in your LinkedIn feed,
like the deceptive weed itself, complete
with sultry, slim and dark-maned Scottish actor –
'I had a love affair with tulips once' –
kitted out in dark brown roll neck sweater?

His bearded lips could just as well be made for
'Why stick to jewels, furs and works of art?
The odd slave thrown in to clean and dust them,
just the ticket. And if you can afford them,
the change will pay for the slave.' Best not
get paranoid. Or do get paranoid.
Think of Lucile at the end of *Danton's Death*:

she's witnessed her lover's public execution –
'And yet there is something serious in it.
I must think … It can't be allowed to happen.'
She sits on the ground, covers her eyes and screams
till everything stops. Uncovers her eyes.
Nothing has stopped. Then think yourself past
Lucile's 'We shall just have to put up with it'.

'But they would have the rabbit out of hiding,
To please the yelping dogs.' – Frost's 'Mending Wall'

Not Another Lockdown Poem

Two years running without palms. No ready
supplies. Saint James in Marylebone,
usually a reliable source, had none in stock.
But wasn't this pushing it after Low Sunday,
a full seventeen days past the main event?

You snuck in before daily mass was due to start,
a handful of worshippers undisturbed
by your entry, looked in the obvious places
and made a swift departure empty handed,
aside from the gift of sanitising gel.

So no replacements for the faded cream
cruciform fronds wedged on the kitchen calendar,
the icon of John the Baptist by the light switch,
the Lord's Prayer nailed to the wardrobe side,
its Gothic lettering undecipherable.

A fox scurried past the kitchen window,
a perfect patch of alopecia on its haunches,
aware not of mange as imminent doom,
only of excruciating itch instead
that impelled it abroad in daylight hours.

Foxes, as far as one can tell, know nothing
of friendship, philosophy, ends and means,
or homosexual love come to that
(thus Lucian), but why should a fox be cast as
any the less conscious? Or a donkey bearing God?

On this year's online census return,
the answers confidential for a century,
you got to the section on religion,
surveyed the options top to bottom,
looked in vain for a box 'Professed by foxes'.

Ricordi

In this last autumn of her life she received with joy a card [Lawrence] sent her from Wellington, addressed to her c/o Ottoline and inscribed with a single word, 'Ricordi!'

Claire Tomalin, *Katherine Mansfield: A Secret Life*

All year long
she had carried them
like weights in the mind
her thoughts of love

when his postcard arrived
from Wellington
care of another
with one word 'Ricordi!'

so in speaking to her
and not to her
he made for the mind
some other atlas

which showed up the strata
and faults of feeling
and lifted a weight
crushing unguarded joy

Golden Moments

Everything we look upon is blest.

W. B. Yeats, 'Vacillation', IV

Yeats, just turned fifty, sat with an empty tea-cup
in a London Lyons Corner House, gazing
on passers-by outside. While I, just turned
sixty-seven, was perched on a stone wall
in Newington Green, watching the kids
and parents in the slanting evening sunshine.
In my case, no cup: the coffee stall was closed.

No one can be denied their golden moments.
According to Yeats, his lasted twenty minutes
'more or less': while he gazed his body, rhyming,
'of a sudden blazed'. This may have taken him
well beyond the average. And if the image
of Yeats sharing a cuppa with the hoi polloi
raises an eyebrow, he was his own judge surely.

Mine lasted sixty seconds 'more or less'
(I don't suppose that Yeats was clock-watching
either), during which time a Red Admiral
sat on my shirt sleeve, perfectly balanced, still,
in exquisite trust. Any blessings going
were due my varifocals. Black, red and white
it blazed. My body was emblazoned with it.

The Mouth, the Face and the Mind

For Rupert

Title of a book by Charlotte Feinman (1999) that 'reviews the dramatic
disorders that present in the head and face'

Too good a title for a medical text, you state.
But then so is *The Piggle*, that key event
in children's literature, the *Attachment
and Loss* trilogy by Bowlby, pure Beckett,
Envy and Gratitude, the darker recesses
of Austen in that one. *The Origins
of Love and Hate*: if only a Victorian
novel had handled Suttie's processes.
Even Bion's blandly titled teasing brew
Experiences in Groups had you laughing
quietly to yourself: 'He really got it.'
Sitting there on a wild and windy evening
reading Freud, what has become of you?
Who are the people you let near your head?

The Summoning

For Andrea

La niebla, aún más cerrada,
exigía partir. Yo tenía los ojos velados por las lágrimas.

Francisco Brines, 'La última costa'

Clearing our mother's flat was a task for
more than one person, not for Augean clutter,
unlikely disputes over who'd get what,
or fear of desecration: no, it was
the feeling that her not being there,
not walking in, would be the more diluted.

Infringements of bedside cabinets,
indignities of looking under wardrobes …
'So that's what …', 'You remember this?': possessions
not hidden exactly, more stowed, a taste
shaped not so much by choice as what was given.
Whatever came in, seldom if ever left.

A therapist friend once stated the idea
that groups can generate what feels like magic,
adding the rider, 'powerful magic' –
something real can come into the room,
circumventing the usual points of entry,
and not through any sacramental presence.

He wasn't speaking about cheap tricks
or making objects appear by means of
one's will, or so it seemed. Quite the reverse,
the ordinary real is magical enough,
bypassing the walls, the windows and door:
the event a mystery, not mystical.

Next time she comes into a room, alone,
will be if or when human reason tumbles.
She'll sidestep walls, vents, windows, ceiling, door,
eyes veiled by tears, urging us to depart.
She'll clasp our hands, we'll hear her native accent
grown stronger in the intervening years.

She'll mention that a strange dream so annoyed her
she upped and walked out of the frame
and broke the necessary illusion.
She is and is not, the magical fusion
untouched by tactics that would avoid her,
her and her expectant uncalled name.

Horse Head of the Moon Goddess

He'd been the chauffeur to celebrities,
dragging the stars to their dawn demise
and unwilling sleep: the coke-flared nostrils,
the backseat shenanigans, the Gucci shades
veiling the opening of the morning's eye.
Twelve-hour shifts made for a dizzy arc
from selenite rise to see the boss tucked in.
Stanco da morire – but not just yet.
Dexterity and grace sufficed the final mile.

White Night

Ах, дверь не запирала я,
Не зажигала свеч,
Не знаешь, как, усталая,
Я не решалась лечь.

Anna Akhmatova, 'White Night'

Ah, I haven't locked the door,
I haven't lit the candles,
you don't know how tired I am,
I haven't the strength to lie down ...

That was as far as she'd got with her 'White Night'.
To halt it there sounded like she was inviting
a mishap or two. A drowsy numbness
pained her sense but didn't snuff the awareness
that the house could easily go up in flames,
prowlers gain entry, swipe the family gems.
Or had she lost the sense, along with the rhymes,
not least the internal? This was no night-time
ennui, no *stanca da morire* mood.
She daren't summon the strength to lie down, stood
upright past exhaustion, the telegraphed lines
bare annotations, the surest of signs
she was wide awake, registering the scene
inside and out, the simplest words no screen.

Seeing how the pine-needles' streaks
fade in the sunset's gloom,
drunk on the sound of a voice
uncannily like that of yours.

And to know that all is lost,
to know that life is hell:
I'm drunk on your voice in the doorway.
I was certain you would come back.

She baulked at the rest, a gloomy sunset
glimpsed through pine-needles, sounds from his throat
that hit her like neat vodka,
the 'All is lost', the 'Life is hell' love trauma.
To freeze frame her in that instant, door unbolted,
candles still unlit, it couldn't be faulted.

But the line Не знаешь, как, усталая
detained her: the enforced commas. To mark a
breath before and after? Did the commas
intensify the moment's inner drama?

Akh, Anna, he could feel, how, tired she was
from a distance of some hundred plus years,
in a language no less liquid than his.
What brought it home were the *shas*, the *zhes*.

Black Stone on a White Stone

For my parents

Me moriré en París con aguacero,
un día del cual tengo ya el recuerdo.
Me moriré en París -y no me corro-
tal vez un jueves, como es hoy, de otoño.

César Vallejo, 'Piedra negra sobre una piedra blanca'

We will depart on an evening in Zone 6,
that much is certain, on a winter's day,
a Thursday or a Friday, that much
we can already remember. It will
not be a weekend but a working day.
'I am the way, the truth and the life':
no turning back to see ourselves alone.
Incise these words on the smooth black stone.
Frances Nolan's brother the mason
has both text and image, white on black,
and will ensure keen chiselling, in instalments.
Pray he be there on both occasions,
not just when one of us takes precedence,
and that his grip not fail him. And looking
backwards and forwards, an acquired skill
of the dearly departed, let not the rain
and solitude have the final word,
be final witnesses, call forth the gesture
that requires a fitting marriage of contrasts,
not as in black and white (the Adélie penguin
who is our guardian in the underworld,
svelte harbinger of cold southern currents
that never carried us both now bears that
particular burden of strange binaries),
more green and turquoise, or red and maroon,

shades that are close together on the spectrum,
each year a libation of tea and whiskey,
enough to moisten the dry soil of March,
the point between our several departures,
and not just any old, the strongest, finest.

Where I Live

Seven, ten, thirty-three, eighty-six – zenith –
thence down to twenty-two, and three: the numbers
of successive flats I have been housed in.
Their rise and fall, expansion-contraction,
I view less as the turn of fortune's wheel
or Cook's Tour from Big Bang to Big Crunch,

more as a classic bell-shaped curve, tailing off
towards zero. At times I see myself
propped up against a wall outdoors, and holding
a placard with no data on me and mine
save for these six figures. As if my mind
sought a fateful framing in their digits.

Numbers at one with the objects they intend,
invoking a knock-down, sightless pageant
of universal domiciles, a tenant
of odds and evens, two of them prime,
a serious candidate for fuzzy logic,
bump function, or the Witch of Agnesi.

But Gaussian distribution admits
of more than one interpretation, surely.
Lockdown strolls take me past three local plaques:
George Orwell, Louis MacNeice, Joe Orton,
known and not known for their longevity.
They flatlined much too soon, their curves too sheer.

Yet what postcode fields a comparable team?
Whose names would I rather wear on my back?
I've lived the past thirty-eight years on the line,
even survived neighbours from hell (Blair, Johnson),
and still feel no urge to N1 elegiacs.
Odds are 3 to 1 I'll be staying put.

Notes

'Grito hacia la Torre del Crysler Building (desde Islington)': the title retains Lorca's misspelling of the building in his 'Grito hacia Roma (desde la torre del Crysler Building)' in *Poeta en Nueva York*.

'Chrysleriana II': phrases in Spanish translate as 'Men should use condoms in their sexual relations' and 'It's possible you have AIDS already and don't know it.'

'Impersonating a Cuckoo': Sophia Loren's films *Boccaccio '70* and *Pane, amore e ...*; 'oompah oompah' (W. H. Auden, 'Music is International'); 'ting a ling ling' (T. S. Eliot, 'Sweeney Agonistes').

'Homage to Isabel Rawsthorne': in writing this sequence, I am greatly indebted to Carol Jacobi's *Out of the Cage: The Art of Isabel Rawsthorne* (2021). Jacobi's extensive research retrieves and illuminates the signal achievements of this artist and intellectual: 'Isabel's career is a missing link that brings to life some of the most exhilarating international dialogues in twentieth-century art' (page 403). These poems try to enter into a more modest, local dialogue with some of Rawsthorne's remarkable canvases and will, I hope, encourage the reader to seek out the originals in galleries or reproduced online as well as in Jacobi's splendidly illustrated book.

'The Desert, 1948-50': 'How revealing it is to see people from a distance'; 'dark green light at midday'; and 'not [...] which is the easel picture' – the artist, quoted in Jacobi, pages 215-16.

'Untitled (Owl), c. 1950-60': words in italics occur in W. B. Yeats's 'Leda and the Swan'.

'Baboon, 1960': this poem draws on ideas and expressions of Vinciane Despret in her essay 'Do Chimpanzees Die Like We Do?', included in *What Would Animals Say If We Asked the Right Questions?* (2016).

'Stoats and Moon, c. 1985': 'no swallow in the stack sign me to leap' – the artist, quoted in Jacobi, page 391.

'Sparrowhawk, c. 1990': 'the characters of the people I have loved touch me with their hands' – the artist, quoted in Jacobi, page 393.

www.ingramcontent.com/pod-product-compliance
Lightning Source LLC
Chambersburg PA
CBHW071446030726
47593CB00003B/918